MAJOR INVENTIONS THROUGH HISTORY

THE HISTORY OF WEAPONS

Judith Herbst

TFCB

TWENTY-FIRST CENTURY BOOKS

Minneapolis

Twenty-First Century Books
A division of Lerner Publishing Group
241 First Avenue North
Minneapolis, MN 55401 U.S.A.

Website address: www.lernerbooks.com

j623.4
Her   OCLC 8/10/06

Library of Congress Cataloging-in-Publication Data

Herbst, Judith.
     The history of weapons / by Judith Herbst.
        p.   cm. — (Major inventions through history)
     Includes bibliographical references and index.
     ISBN-13: 978—0—8225—3805—9
     ISBN-10: 0—8225—3805—9 (lib. bdg. : alk. paper)
     I. Military weapons—History—Juvenile literature. I. Title. II. Series.
  U800.H47 2006
  623.4—dc22   2004025267

Manufactured in the United States of America
1 2 3 4 5 6 — DP — 11 10 09 08 07 06

CONTENTS

Introduction

Human beings have always used weapons. From the earliest times, we used them to protect ourselves and to hunt for food. But mostly we have used weapons against each other—for power, land, religion, and riches. This fact can make the history of weapons both fascinating and uncomfortable.

At first, our weapons were simple. Early humans simply picked up what was nearby, such as rocks or sharp sticks. Fighting was personal—we had to be within throwing distance of our enemy. But gradually, we learned to develop more efficient and destructive weapons. In modern times, wars are fought on huge battlefields, on the sea, and in the air.

So how did we get from sticks and stones to weapons of mass destruction? Read on.

CHAPTER 1

Guns

When we picture a gun, we usually think of bullets or cartridges. So why are handguns and rifles often called firearms? Where's the fire? Well, early in our history, we actually did hurl flaming globs of stuff at each other. These weapons weren't guns, but they were certainly firearms, and they eventually led to the development of guns.

In the seventh century A.D., Greeks living in the Byzantine Empire (the land surrounding the eastern Mediterranean Sea) probably had the most effective firearm in the ancient world. It was created by an architect named Callinicus, who was born in Syria around 620. Callinicus's invention came to be known as Greek fire.

Greek fire might be described as a gigantic flaming bullet. The Greeks filled clay pots with a secret mixture and flung them at enemy troops. They also used brass tubes to spray enemy ships with Greek fire. According to legend, the stuff caught fire spontaneously and was almost impossible to put out—even with water!

Greek fire could set ships aflame and kill large numbers of warriors with a single shot. Shields and armor were useless against the flames. Clearly, the army that had Greek fire had the upper hand.

The Byzantine emperor Constantine IV realized this, and he closely guarded the formula for making the deadly mixture. It was never written down, so no one knows exactly what was used. But historians think Greek fire included flammable chemicals and minerals such as liquid petroleum, pitch (a tar residue), saltpeter (potassium nitrate), and sulfur. Those are some of the same ingredients found in the next big idea—gunpowder.

First Shots

Around 850 some Chinese inventors were mixing minerals and chemicals, searching for a potion that would bring eternal life. Instead, they came up with gunpowder.

The Chinese produced gunpowder with saltpeter, sulfur, and carbon (the black, sooty stuff left after wood is burned). All these

Callinicus Invents
Greek fire.
A.D. 600s

Chinese chemists
invent gunpowder.
850

materials are safe by themselves. But put them together and throw in a source of fire, and the mixture turns to gas so quickly that it creates an explosion.

The Chinese experimented with exploding gunpowder inside a cylinder, or narrow tube. They found that the explosion created enough force to shoot an object out of the cylinder. Shortly before 1000, the Chinese designed what is probably the world's first gun. It was a piece of bamboo (a strong, hollow reed) that fired a small spear. The Chinese soon saw the military value of what they had discovered.

A SECRET RECIPE

In the 1200s, the English scholar Roger Bacon almost blew himself up when he mixed together the ingredients that produce gunpowder. So when Bacon wrote down the recipe, he used a secret code to prevent "the uneducated" from getting their hands on it. It took 650 years to crack the code.

By the early 1300s, guns were starting to show up on the battlefields of Europe. But the guns were hard to use and often dangerous. The gunpowder had to be poured in and then ignited. So the shooter always had to carry around a fire source, called a touch paper, to set off the gunpowder. (See why they were called firearms?) Unexpected explosions were common because nobody really knew how much gunpowder to pour down the barrel.

As the years passed, inventors kept working on ways to improve firearms. The matchlock gun was introduced around 1450. It had a

Chinese inventors
design the first gun.
ca. 1000

Roger Bacon writes down
the formula for gunpowder.
1200s

The soldier in this drawing is carrying a matchlock gun.

little S-shaped piece of metal called a serpentine, a kind of early trigger. One end of the serpentine held a fuse that burned slowly. The shooter pulled back on the other end of the serpentine, bringing the fuse to the gunpowder. The slow fuse was an improvement over previous ignition systems, or ways to light the gunpowder.

Even with improvements, guns of this period were still trouble to operate. Shooters had to go through the complicated reloading process after every shot. Taking accurate aim was also difficult. Bullets were not uniform in shape, and there was no real way to control the speed or exact direction of the bullet as it traveled down and out of the barrel.

Cannons and guns are used
on European battlefields.
1300s

The matchlock gun
is introduced.
1450

A Turning Point

Around 1515 the wheel lock made its appearance. The wheel lock made shooting a lot easier, especially in bad weather, because it did away with the need for a fire source. The gunpowder was ignited by friction created by the spin of a little wheel inside the gun. The wheel lock was reliable, but it was also expensive. It became popular with private gun owners but wasn't used by the military. It simply cost too much money to supply an entire army with wheel locks.

The flintlock musket, introduced in 1610, proved the worth of guns as battlefield weapons. A musket is heavy, fired from the shoulder, and muzzle-loaded

Muskets *(right)* were very common weapons for soldiers and hunters. But they weren't very reliable. They often could not hit a target more than 50 yards (45 meters) away.

The wheel lock is invented.
1515

Marin le Bourgeoys invents the flintlock.
1610

(meaning that the powder and ammunition are loaded from the muzzle, or the front of the barrel). The flintlock version was designed by Marin le Bourgeoys of Normandy (France). Improvements made it safe, easy to use, very reliable, and fairly cheap. In a short time, it became standard military equipment all around the world. Because the flintlock could be used by almost anyone, even peasants and farmers could join the fighting ranks.

Muskets were the standard weapons of foot soldiers and hunters for almost two centuries. But by the late 1700s, another type of weapon was gaining popularity—the rifle. To make a rifle, gunsmiths (gun makers) cut spiral grooves along the insides of gun barrels. Called rifling, the grooves put a spin on the bullet, which greatly improved firing accuracy and distance.

LEATHER GUNS

Sometime around 1620, gunsmiths in Europe introduced leather guns. The guns were popular for a while because they were half the weight of a metal gun. Unfortunately, they used twice as much gunpowder and wore out a lot faster.

During the American Revolution (1775–1783), rifles became the weapon of choice among the colonists fighting the British army. American riflemen developed a lethal reputation for their skill and long-range accuracy. The superiority of American rifles over British muskets helped the colonists win their independence.

Leather guns are introduced.
1620

Rifles help colonists win the American Revolution.
1775–1783

During the American Revolution, British and colonial soldiers fought a battle with rifles and muskets in the town square of Lexington, Massachusetts, on April 19, 1775.

This same period saw a new improvement in ammunition. Most soldiers began carrying ammunition in the form of cartridges. These cartridges were paper packets containing a lead ball (the projectile) and a measured amount of gunpowder. To load a rifle, the soldier bit off an end of the cartridge, poured the gunpowder down the barrel, and then rammed the ball and paper into the barrel. This was much faster and easier than measuring out powder for every shot.

An amendment to the U.S. Constitution guarantees citizens the right to bear arms.

1787

The U.S. Congress establishes the Springfield (Massachusetts) Armory.

1794

Revolvers

By the mid-1800s, the demand for guns was huge. The U.S. military had its own armory, or place for making and storing guns. But several private gun manufacturers had also established themselves in the United States and Europe.

In 1835 American Samuel Colt received a patent (a legal claim to an invention) for a handgun. Colt's gun had a revolving cylinder that held six bullets, so it became known as a revolver, or a six-shooter. Each time the gun was fired, the cylinder revolved to put another bullet in firing position. The gun could fire six times before the shooter had to stop to reload. Colt won contracts to supply his revolver to the British army and navy.

Colt's invention was improved by the development of

THE FERGUSON RIFLE

During the American Revolution, the colonists' Kentucky rifle outshot the British Brown Bess musket time and again. So the British army worked on getting out its own rifle model. It was called the Ferguson rifle, after its inventor, Patrick Ferguson.

Ferguson designed his firearm after a French model, adding improvements for accuracy. At a demonstration for British army commanders, Ferguson fired four shots per minute, hitting his target every time from a distance of 200 yards (183 m). And he did it all in heavy rain and wind. The British immediately put Ferguson in charge of the special training of one hundred riflemen. But luckily for the colonists, the Ferguson rifle never made it into battle. In September 1777, Ferguson was seriously wounded by a colonist's bullet. Without his leadership, the unit of riflemen was recalled.

Samuel Colt applies for a patent for his revolver.

1835

more effective cartridges. In 1847 a French gunsmith, B. Houlier, patented a new type of metal cartridge that fired when struck on its base. This cartridge was an early form of the modern-day bullet.

In 1856 Massachusetts gunsmiths Horace Smith and Daniel Wesson introduced their own version of the revolver. Smith and Wesson began manufacturing their gun just in time for the American Civil War (1861–1865). Officers and soldiers on both sides of the conflict carried revolvers.

During the Civil War, another breakthrough weapon was developed—the repeating rifle. Repeating rifles, such as the Henry repeating rifle, held as many as fifteen cartridges. After firing, the shooter simply cocked the handle to reload. The repeating rifle gave Northern troops a huge advantage over Southern troops, who still used slower-loading weapons.

More than fifty types of rifles were used during the Civil War. The number of guns used, the effectiveness of new and more accurate weapons, inexperienced soldiers, and a lack of medical care on the battlefield helped make the Civil War the deadliest conflict yet in American history—with 620,000 casualties.

The Wild West

Guns played a big part in settling the American West. As pioneers moved over the Great Plains and the Rocky Mountains in the

B. Houlier patents an early
form of the bullet.
1847

1800s, they needed guns for hunting and for protecting themselves out in the middle of nowhere.

But in some Western towns and settlements, guns weren't used so sparingly. Parts of the West were truly wild and lawless, and everyone carried revolvers and rifles. Sheriffs, of course, had guns. But so did outlaws, who used guns to rob banks, stagecoaches, and trains. Ranchers, stagecoach drivers, gamblers, cowboys, cattlemen, and even little old ladies in bonnets carried firearms. There were few laws regarding guns, and if you had the money, you could buy one.

Guns were also used to take western lands away from Native Americans.

The cover of this dime-store novel from the 1930s about the outlaw Jesse James depicts a Wild West shootout in the 1800s.

Smith and Wesson
introduce their revolver.
1856

The U.S. government and pioneers wanted Native American lands for farms and ranches. Some Native American groups were attacked and killed or driven off their traditional territories. Frontiersmen also began shooting buffalo by the thousands, taking away the Native Americans' main source of food. Many Native American groups fought back, but they were usually no match for the U.S. Army.

Not-So-Friendly Fire

As we've seen, guns have been used to fight wars and gain more territory. They've been used to push people off their lands. But they've also been used to help people win their freedom during rebellions, as they did during the American Revolution. They've helped people protect themselves and be self-sufficient.

But some people question the need for guns in a modern society. We don't have to hunt for food anymore. We have laws and law officers to protect us. We have government agencies and worldwide organizations to help settle problems between countries or groups of people.

Yet more than sixty-five million people in the United States are registered gun owners. Among them, they own at least 200 million firearms. Some of these gun owners hunt for sport. Some keep guns in their homes for self-defense. Others are collectors interested in gun history and technology.

But many guns wind up in the hands of criminals. In other cases, children find guns in their homes and accidentally shoot themselves or someone else. These illegal and accidental uses of guns have led some people to question whether it is too easy to get a gun in the United States. They urge the government to put more controls on who owns and carries guns. On the other side of the argument, gun owners say that their right to bear arms (or own weapons) is guaranteed by the U.S. Constitution. More than one thousand years after the invention of gunpowder, the debate on gun control continues.

A PERFECT MATCH

Every time a gun is fired, it leaves its own special signature on the bullet. As the bullet shoots through the barrel, it picks up scratches from the gun's spiral grooves. The scratch patterns are unique to each gun. Even guns that look exactly alike on the outside have slightly different spiral grooving on the inside. So bullets can tell police quite a story about where they've been.

If a bullet is recovered from a crime scene or removed from a victim, it is sent to a police lab. If police have found the weapon they think was used in the crime, they fire that gun and send that bullet to the lab too. Scientists then examine both bullets under side-by-side microscopes. If the markings match, it means the bullets came from the same gun.

CHAPTER 2
Dynamite and TNT

As far back as the eleventh century, the Chinese knew that gunpowder exploded rather nicely. In 1427 Italians poured some into an earthenware pot, lit it, and invented the first hand grenade. A hand grenade is basically a bomb that is small enough to throw at someone.

During the American Revolution, soldiers used lemon-sized hand grenades made of cast iron. The grenades had an opening at the top for the gunpowder and a smaller one on the side for the

Italians invent the
first hand grenade.
1427

wick. Damage wasn't caused so much by the explosion as by the fragments of flying metal, known as shrapnel, that resulted.

A Turtle Takes on the British

Two other very important military inventions made their debuts during the American Revolution. The first was a small, enclosed boat that traveled under water. This first submarine was designed and built by American David Bushnell in 1775. The second invention was the explosive device that Bushnell stowed on board.

Bushnell's one-man submarine was called the *Turtle*, and it carried a gunpowder bomb. The *Turtle*'s mission was to blow up a British warship that lay anchored in New York Harbor. Unfortunately, Ezra Lee, the *Turtle*'s pilot, couldn't attach the bomb to the side of the warship. He had to abandon the bomb.

Although the mission failed, the *Turtle* set the stage for a deadly pairing—the submarine and the torpedo. More than one hundred years after the *Turtle*, the submarine and the torpedo would revolutionize warfare at sea. But for that to happen, inventors had to develop much more powerful explosives.

Nitroglycerin

In 1846 Italian chemist Ascanio Sobrero created an oily mixture that he called pyroglycerin. He wasn't quite sure what it was until he tried heating it in a little test tube. A few moments later, the stuff

American rebels use a
submarine to try to blow up
a British warship.

1775

Ascanio Sobrero
invents nitroglycerin.

1846

exploded with such violence that almost everyone in Sobrero's lab was wounded. Sobrero immediately decided that pyroglycerin was too dangerous to be useful.

A young Swedish engineer, Alfred Nobel, didn't agree. In 1849 he saw a laboratory demonstration of pyroglycerin (called nitroglycerin by this time). Nobel recognized the substance's potential for construction projects, such as blasting holes for tunnels. But in its present form, the explosive couldn't be safely manufactured, packaged, transported, or used. If you jostled it, it exploded. If it got too hot, it exploded. And it never reacted the same way twice. So, in 1863, Nobel started experimenting with ways to stabilize nitroglycerin.

Alfred Nobel

Dynamite

Nobel discovered that if he mixed an absorbent material such as sand with the nitroglycerin, it wouldn't explode on its own. The mixture could be shaped into rods with fuses on one end. Nobel called his invention dynamite (from a Greek word meaning "power"). In 1867 he received a patent for it.

Alfred Nobel receives a
patent for dynamite.
1867

Dynamite soon went to war. Soldiers still fought each other on the battlefield, but dynamite made it easier to try to defeat the enemy in other ways. Armies would dynamite roads, bridges, and railroads to slow down enemy troops. Armies also tried to hit enemy supply depots—buildings where food and ammunition were stored.

THE NOBEL PRIZE

Alfred Nobel had developed dynamite for construction, not for war. When Nobel died in 1896, he left instructions that most of his large fortune should be used to reward people who work for the benefit of humanity. Since 1901 Nobel prizes have been awarded every year in the fields of physics, chemistry, medicine, literature, and peace.

TNT

After dynamite, TNT was the next big explosives invention. TNT stands for trinitrotoluene. Trinitrotoluene had been used in industry for many years, but it wasn't used as an explosive until 1904. A little gentle heating turns the TNT crystals into a liquid so it can be poured into shells—ammunition for artillery (large, heavy guns).

During World War I (1914–1918), the British army developed a new weapon called a tank. A tank is a heavy vehicle plated with metal armor. It can roll over barbed wire fences and withstand enemy gunfire. To battle these tough vehicles, both sides developed antitank mines, or bombs planted in the ground. Mines are detonated, or set off, by pressure. Antitank mines exploded when

TNT is used as an explosive
for the first time.
1904

LAND MINES

Land mines can injure or kill civilians (nonmilitary people) even years after a conflict ends. After a war is over, unexploded land mines are left behind, hidden beneath roads and fields. Anyone can accidentally step on a land mine—children walking to school or a farmer planting crops. In the early 2000s, there were 110 million unexploded land mines in the world, buried in sixty-eight countries from Vietnam to Nicaragua. Every year, twenty thousand people step on mines and are either killed or seriously injured. The African country of Angola alone has seventy thousand land mine amputees (people who have lost arms and legs). Most of the amputees are children. Many governments and international agencies, such as the International Red Cross and the United Nations, have worked to ban the production and sale of land mines. They also work to clear areas of mines by safely detonating the explosives.

tanks rolled over them. To make sure the resulting explosion was strong enough to damage the tank, mine makers used TNT.

TNT was also used in torpedoes. A torpedo is basically a self-propelled underwater bomb. It can be launched from a submarine at an enemy ship thousands of yards away. Powered by an engine, the torpedo cruises beneath the water's surface until it hits an enemy ship. A torpedo can leave a hole in the side of the ship as big as a barn door.

To fight submarines, the British came up with the depth charge. The depth charge was basically a big drum filled with TNT. Sailors rolled it off the side of a ship, and when the drum reached a certain depth, it exploded. A depth charge almost never hit a submarine directly.

A German submarine torpedoes the passenger ship *Lusitania*, killing twelve hundred civilians.

1915

German submarines sink 430 enemy ships with torpedoes.

1917

U.S. Coast Guardsmen aboard the ship *Spencer* watch a depth-charge explosion during World War II.

But the blast would loosen the submarine's joints and damage its instruments, forcing the submarine to surface. By World War II (1939–1945), submarines carried many torpedoes with powerful warheads, while battleships carried depth charges.

But TNT played an even bigger role on land during World War II. By this time, long-range aircraft were able to take the war far behind the battle lines. The British Royal Air Force (RAF), U.S.

A U.S. Corsair fighter plane fires rockets on enemy Japanese forces in the South Pacific island of Okinawa during World War II.

Army Air Force (USAAF), and the German Luftwaffe (air force) sent waves of aircraft loaded with TNT bombs over enemy cities and industrial areas. Since it was difficult for the high-flying aircraft to achieve pinpoint accuracy, the planes simply dropped their bombs on an entire area. These bombing campaigns were designed to cripple the enemy's ability to produce war materials and to break the will of the enemy population. The practice caused widespread death and destruction and affected civilians a way never before seen in history. The campaigns

The German air force begins bombing London and southern England.

1940

The RAF and USAAF bomb the German city of Dresden.

1945

helped U.S. and British forces to defeat Germany and Japan, but war would never be the same again.

Since the 1950s, dynamite has been replaced by other high explosives, or explosives that detonate very fast. But nitroglycerin and TNT, often mixed with other chemicals, are still used in construction, demolition, and warfare.

SMART BOMBS

Precision-guided munitions, known as smart bombs, are bombs fitted with special guidance equipment. Smart bombs use laser beams, infrared sensing devices, TV cameras, or even navigation signals from satellites to find a very specific target. A military force can use a small number of smart bombs to destroy enemy targets without bombing an entire area.

The U.S. military uses smart bombs in Iraq against Saddam Hussein's troops.
1990–1991

CHAPTER 3

Automatic Weapons

Before 1862, shooting at somebody required a lot of patience. Load, aim, shoot. Load, aim, shoot. And if the other guy loaded, aimed, and shot faster than you, your future was not bright. The repeating rifle and the Colt revolver sped things up a bit, but you still only got a handful of shots before you had to reload. Then along came Richard Gatling of North Carolina with the first successful rapid-fire weapon—a gun that mechanically reloaded itself.

Richard Gatling invents the
first machine gun.
1862

Rapid Fire

Gatling was not a military man or a hunter. He was an inventor who had designed a number of grain-sowing machines and equipment for steamboats. But when the American Civil War broke out, Gatling turned his attention to firearms.

The Gatling gun has six to ten rifle barrels that rotate, or move in a circle, around a central shaft. The gun operator turns the shaft with a hand crank. As each barrel reaches the top position of the rotation, ammunition drops in from a storage drum. When the loaded barrel reaches the bottom of the rotation, it fires. The empty ammunition shell is spit out, and the barrel continues on its rotation, ready to be reloaded. The Gatling gun fires hundreds of rounds per minute, mowing down dozens of enemy troops. In the last half of the nineteenth century, the Gatling gun turned many battles into slaughters.

The Machine Gun

In 1883 Hiram Maxim invented the first automatic weapon. The Gatling gun was rapid-fire but not automatic. Maxim's machine gun was both.

An automatic weapon fires continuously as long as the trigger is held down. The Maxim machine gun used the energy created by each shot to push another round into place and cock the trigger again. It shot six hundred rounds a minute and was very easy to fire. All you had to do was pull back on the trigger and hold it there. The gun did the rest.

Hiram Maxim invents the
first automatic weapon.
1883

World War I came to be called the machine-gun war because every country involved in the fighting had some version of the automatic weapon. But these big, heavy guns were hard to move, so the gunners couldn't follow the action. They couldn't attack. But aircraft carrying machine guns could and did—and that added a whole new dimension to war.

World War I was the first time airplanes were used in combat. The planes of this era were made of wood, with small engines and an open cockpit. At first, the planes were used for reconnaissance. They flew over enemy territory to see what the enemy forces were doing. But soon people found a way to use them as offensive weapons. Machine guns were bolted just outside the cockpit, and pilots fired as they flew. Fighter pilots, such as

A German pilot drops a bomb during World War I.

The Colt .38 pistol becomes an official U.S. military firearm.

1911

Manfred Freiherr von Richthofen came to be known as the Red Baron because he flew a red Fokker triplane. During World War I, he shot down eighty enemy aircraft. But machine-gun fire from the ground finally knocked Richthofen out of the sky before the war ended.

Germany's famous Manfred Freiherr von Richthofen, also known as the Red Baron, sprayed battlefields, as well as other planes, with machine-gun fire.

The Machine Gun Loses Weight

In 1917 the German army was trying to capture the city of Riga in Latvia, a country between the Baltic Sea and Russia. But the Russians beat back the Germans in a bloody fight. So German army general Oskar von Hutier came up with a bold new plan—infiltrate. His idea was to break up his army into small fighting groups and have them sneak through gaps in the enemy lines. Then they could spread out and attack. But such a maneuver would be impossible to do with heavy, awkward machine guns.

PROHIBITION

In 1920 the Eighteenth Amendment to the U.S. Constitution went into effect. The amendment prohibited, or outlawed, the production and sale of almost all alcoholic beverages. The new law came to be called Prohibition. But instead of ending irresponsible drinking, Prohibition mostly created a huge market for illegal liquor.

Criminals such as Al Capone and Bugs Moran made fortunes illegally importing liquor from other countries and selling it in the United States. The competition in this criminal market led to gang wars and murder, and the weapon of choice was the tommy gun. It was small enough to hide and powerful enough to mow down a group of rival criminals from a distance. There was often little the police could do to control gangsters with their tommy guns.

Clearly, the troops needed a smaller machine gun.

It just so happened that Hugo Schmeisser of Germany had already designed such a gun. Schmeisser's Bergmann Mashinen Pistole 18 was a *sub*machine gun— the first of its kind. It was an automatic gun, but it used pistol ammunition. It could fire four hundred rounds a minute and was less than 3 feet (1 m) long. But best of all, it only weighed 14 pounds (6 kilograms). Soldiers could carry it with just a handy leather strap. Von Hutier and his army used the submachine gun to break through enemy lines several times in the spring of 1918.

Other Rapid-Fire Guns

In 1920 John Thompson produced his own submachine gun. Thompson had been a general in

Hugo Schmeisser designs the Bergmann Mashinen Pistole 18.

1917

Prohibition-era gangsters with tommy guns made popular movie villains.

the U.S. Army during World War I, and he designed his gun for the battlefields of Europe. During World War II, his submachine gun, which came to be called the tommy gun, became the standard weapon for many U.S. soldiers. By this time, new strategies relied on infiltration, just as von Hutier had suggested thirty years earlier. Lightweight submachine guns were needed on both sides.

John Thompson invents
the tommy gun.
1920

STURMGEWEHR

During World War II, Hugo Schmeisser introduced the Sturmgewehr, which in German means "storm weapon." The Sturmgewehr was an assault rifle—a gun that can switch from semiautomatic to automatic by just turning a little selector dial. In the last part of the twentieth century, the AK-47 became the most widely used assault rifle in the world.

Soldiers also carried semiautomatic pistols. A semiautomatic gun automatically reloads itself. But to fire, the gun operator has to pull the trigger each time. Both fully automatic and semiautomatic pistols hold several rounds of ammunition in a magazine, sometimes called a clip, which slips into the gun butt.

Modern automatic and semiautomatic pistols can hold three times as much ammunition as a revolver. Thanks to new materials, they are small and lightweight. They have become the most popular military firearms in the world.

CHAPTER 4
Weapons of Mass Destruction

The ultimate war weapon is one that causes mass destruction. Such weapons can kill large numbers of soldiers on the battlefield or civilians in cities in a matter of minutes or even seconds. The weapons can also damage or destroy homes, hospitals, communications centers, transportation systems, and supply centers.

Many weapons of mass destruction (WMD) were invented for warfare in the twentieth century. Some are made from poisonous chemical compounds. Other weapons draw their power from physical processes deep within the core of the bomb, at the level of atoms and nuclei. Still other WMD are biological weapons, which use deadly bacteria, viruses, or fungi. All these new weapons have changed the way wars are fought.

World War I Gases

Thousands of years ago, when an army attacked a city, the soldiers often poured poison into local wells. That simple action took away the enemy's source of drinking water. During World War I, the Germans came up with another idea. They poisoned the air their enemies breathed.

Armies on both sides of the conflict used vaporized chemicals—poisonous chemical compounds in the form of a gas. In 1914 French forces fired tear-gas grenades at German troops. The tear gas irritated enemy soldiers' eyes and caused coughing. In April 1915, the Germans used a much more serious gas against French troops during the Battle of Ypres in northern Belgium.

The Germans first began pounding the French troops with artillery fire. Moments later, two greenish yellow clouds of chlorine gas drifted over the French soldiers. They found themselves struggling to breathe as the gas attacked their throats and lungs. They began to cough violently. Many choked to death in agony.

German soldiers attack
French troops with chlorine
gas at Ypres, Belgium.

1915

The Germans had fired metal canisters full of the chlorine gas, then relied on the wind to carry it over the French troops. The attack shocked the Allies (France, Great Britain, and other countries), and they began to fight back with chlorine gas. Both sides also began to use phosgene, another gas that attacks the respiratory (breathing) system. As the war went on, gas masks (filters worn over the face) became a standard part of military equipment.

In June 1915, British troops received "hypo helmets" *(above)* to protect them against chlorine gas attacks. The helmets were actually bags that fitted over the soldier's head. A piece of plastic served as an eyepiece.

In 1917 the Germans introduced mustard gas. (Its name comes from its mustardlike smell.) Mustard gas causes severe blisters on the skin and inside the body. If inhaled, it attacks lung tissue. By the end of the war, the Germans had killed several hundred thousand Allied soldiers with mustard gas.

World War II

The use of chemical weapons was banned by the Geneva Protocol (agreement) in 1925. But scientists continued to experiment with new and deadlier chemical compounds.

In 1936 German scientist Gerhard Schrader was doing research on insecticides when he came up with a terrible substance. It was so toxic, Schrader found he couldn't even work with it. He called it tabun.

Tabun is a nerve gas. When it is inhaled or absorbed through the skin, it attacks a victim's nervous system (the brain, spinal cord, and network of nerves that control the muscles). If the victim is exposed to enough tabun, every muscle in the body begins to contract. The victim vomits, goes into convulsions, and suffocates to death.

The German army quickly learned of Schrader's discovery. After watching a demonstration of the gas, they ordered tabun into production. Schrader, however, wasn't finished yet. In 1938 he discovered a compound that turned out to be ten times as poisonous as tabun. He named it sarin. A year later, scientists in Berlin, Germany, produced the first batch of sarin gas.

The German military begins using mustard gas against enemy troops.

1917

Geneva Protocol outlaws the use of chemical and biological weapons.

1925

Gerhard Schrader develops tabun.

1936

Sarin continues to be used as a weapon. In 1995 members of the Japanese religious cult Aum Shinrikyo attacked a crowded Tokyo subway train with sarin gas, killing twelve people and injuring thousands.

As World War II began, the Germans built up huge stocks of sarin and tabun gas. They developed gas bombs and rockets and sarin-firing machine guns. The Germans were well prepared to bomb the people of London, England, with these new WMD. But for some reason, Adolf Hitler, the German leader, decided against using these chemical weapons on the battlefield. Instead, the Germans used them on other civilians.

Hitler planned to take over the world and to create a pure-blooded master race. Certain other races and groups, Hitler claimed, were dangerous or inferior and must be eliminated. Hitler hated Jews and targeted them in particular. But he also wanted to

German scientists make the first batch of sarin gas.
1939

get rid of the Roma (a people from eastern Europe), mentally and physically disabled people, his political enemies, and several other groups. Hitler's Nazi troops rounded up people who belonged to these groups. The Nazis shot tens of thousands of them to death. But the Nazis took many more people to concentration camps where the Nazis had built special gas chambers.

The gassing began in 1941 at a small camp in Poland called Gross-Rosen. Soon Nazis were gassing prisoners at the death camps of Treblinka, Belzac, Auschwitz, and Sobibor. Prisoners were marched into what they thought were large shower rooms. Guards bolted the door behind the prisoners and turned the showers on. But instead of water, the showers pumped in Zyklon-B, a form of the deadly gas cyanide. Prisoners began dying within seconds.

The Nazis continued the gassing day after day, month after month, for almost four years. The victims of the Nazi concentration camps number in the millions. Using gas on civilians did not help Hitler create a master race or win the war. The Nazis were defeated in 1945, and Hitler committed suicide. But the Holocaust, as Hitler's mass murder of innocent civilians came to be called, stands as one of history's worst crimes.

The A-Bomb

After Nazi Germany surrendered to the Allies in Europe, World War II still raged in the Pacific Ocean and in Asia. The Allies had

Nazis first use Zyklon-B to gas concentration camp prisoners.

1941

defeated Japan, one of Germany's partners, in several important battles. But Japan refused to surrender completely. The Allies believed that to end the war, they would have to stage a land invasion of Japan. Hundreds of thousands more troops would die in such an invasion.

In the summer of 1945, scientists in the United States successfully tested a new top-secret weapon in the New Mexico desert. That weapon was the atomic bomb (or A-bomb). The A-bomb was the first of its kind—a weapon that used the energy created by splitting the nuclei of atoms. A small A-bomb is equal to the force of 20,000 tons (18,144 metric tons) of TNT.

U.S. president Harry S. Truman told other Allied leaders about the successful test. Three Allied governments—the United States, Great Britain, and China—decided to use the information to threaten Japan. Surrender, they said, or we'll use the A-bomb on Japanese cities. When the Japanese military kept on fighting, Truman decided to carry through on the threat.

On August 6, 1945, at 8:15 A.M., a B-29 bomber called the *Enola Gay* dropped an A-bomb over the city of Hiroshima, Japan. Forty-three seconds later, it exploded, completely wiping out 5 square miles (13 sq. kilometers) of the city's center. The explosion killed seventy thousand people instantly.

When Japan still refused to surrender, the United States dropped a second A-bomb over the city of Nagasaki, Japan, on August 9.

The U.S. military drops
atomic bombs on Japan.

1945

Nagasaki, Japan, after the 1945 A-bomb explosion. The blast destroyed 1.8 miles (2.9 km) of the city center.

This time, forty thousand people were killed. The Japanese government surrendered the following day.

Even after the bombings, many Japanese people continued to die. A-bombs produce huge amounts of energy in the form of intense heat. Many survivors of the initial explosions were badly burned and died later of their injuries. Months and even years later, people died from radiation sickness and cancers caused by nuclear fallout, the poisonous product of an atomic explosion. Fallout also killed crops and animals and poisoned the air, water, and soil.

The Cold War

The end of World War II led to a new war—the Cold War (1945–1991). During World War II, the United States and the Union of Soviet Socialist Republics (USSR) had been allies. But soon after, the governments of the two countries became enemies. The conflict was called a "cold" war because there were no actual battles. But the threat of real war drove what came to be called the nuclear arms race. The Soviets developed their own atomic bomb in 1949. From that point on, the two rivals raced to build more powerful bombs and better ways to deliver them. By the late 1950s, the United States and the USSR had built enough nuclear weapons to destroy life on earth. By the 1960s, both countries had developed intercontinental ballistic missiles (ICBMs) that could carry nuclear warheads thousands of miles to reach targets. This created a situation known as mutual assured destruction, or MAD. A Soviet attack would lead to a U.S. counterattack or vice versa. Either way, both sides would be destroyed.

CRUISE MISSILES

Cruise missiles are among the most advanced weapons in the world. They can carry nuclear warheads and can be launched from the air, on land, or at sea. They have a range of about 700 miles (1,127 km). Cruise missiles are extremely accurate and can be programmed to hit their targets within a few feet. They also fly—or cruise—fast and low. That makes them difficult to detect with radar.

U.S. and Soviet forces come close to nuclear war during the Cuban missile crisis.

1962

In some ways, MAD forced governments to be more careful about dealing with each other. Neither the United States nor the USSR wanted worldwide destruction. But even the threat of nuclear war terrified civilians throughout the 1950s and 1960s. In the United States, families built bomb shelters under their backyards, filling them with years' worth of food. Schoolchildren practiced what to do in case of a nuclear attack. Early-warning sirens were tested each week in neighborhoods across the country.

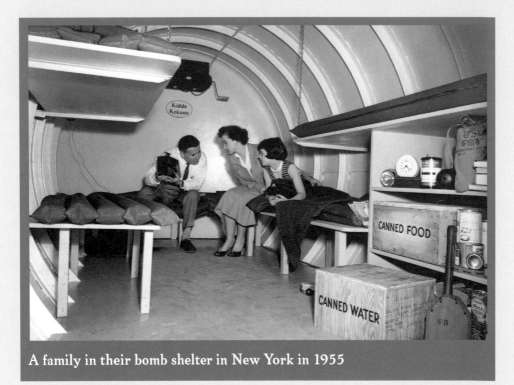

A family in their bomb shelter in New York in 1955

By the 1970s, the Cold War threats were easing, and both the United States and the USSR recognized the need to control the nuclear arms race. In 1970 the Treaty on the Non-Proliferation of Nuclear Weapons went into effect. The treaty was an agreement among almost two hundred nations to control the proliferation (building and distribution) of nuclear weapons. Throughout the 1970s and into the 1980s, the United States and the USSR continued to compete with each other for political power. But they also tried to establish more open relations. The Cold War ended in 1991, when the USSR collapsed and became many separate nations. However, the threat of nuclear attacks remains. Some experts believe it is just a matter of time before terrorists obtain nuclear weapons.

Biological Weapons

Experts also fear what could happen if terrorists attacked using biological weapons of mass destruction. Biological WMD release viruses, or bacteria that cause serious and even deadly diseases, such as anthrax, bubonic

EARLY BIOLOGICAL WEAPONS

Biological weapons are not new. During World War II, Japan used biological weapons against Chinese civilians. Great Britain, the United States, and Germany tested and developed their own biological weapons, although they never used them. And during the Cold War, the United States suspected that the USSR was testing anthrax weapons.

plague, and smallpox. The thought of such WMD is terrifying for most people. According to the U.S. Centers for Disease Control and Prevention, a few kilograms of anthrax spores could prove as deadly as a Hiroshima-size nuclear bomb.

Once the weapon releases the biological matter, victims can touch, swallow, or breathe in the bacteria or virus without realizing it. They can then spread it to other people unknowingly. The effects of the biological WMD become widespread and uncontrolled. Thousands of people in the same area could fall ill at the same time. Emergency services and hospitals would be overwhelmed. And if just one person carrying a virus gets on an airplane, the disease would spread to another city or country.

In the 2000s, the threat of terrorist attacks heightened fears about biological WMD. Some terrorist groups, such as al-Qaeda (which carried out the 2001 attacks on the World Trade Center in New York and the Pentagon near Washington, D.C.), are very large and organized. These terrorist organizations have enough money to buy a lot of guns, and many even run training camps for their members. But terrorist groups are not governments or armies. They don't have countries from which to launch attacks. They don't have airplanes, tanks, and other equipment for fighting battles. Terrorist groups instead often rely on improvised weapons. For example, in the 2001 al-Qaeda attacks on the World Trade Center and the Pentagon, terrorists hijacked commercial airplanes, essentially turning the planes into huge bombs.

Antiterrorism experts worry that biological WMD also could be improvised. Terrorists would have to know how to handle biological agents, such as the smallpox virus or anthrax spores. Some bacteria or viruses can't survive certain temperatures. Others are only effective in one form. But beyond that, staging a biological WMD attack on civilians could be very simple. The biological agent could be sprayed from a crop-dusting plane, dumped into a city's water supply, used to contaminate food, or mailed in letters.

Experts have repeatedly warned that the United States and most other countries are not prepared for a biological attack. Equipment for detecting biological weapons is needed. New medicines should be developed and stockpiled. Medical teams, local police forces, local governments, and disaster relief agencies need more specialized training. In addition to being prepared for attack, experts urge governments to step up efforts to stop terrorists from ever obtaining biological WMD.

A presidential commission reports that the United States is not prepared for a biological attack.

2005

Epilogue

Humans still have many of the same reasons for fighting each other—land, money, religion, and race. But our weapons technology has come a long way. What lies in the future?

Perhaps soon, within the next thirty years, people won't have to fight each other at all. Robots will do it for us. The U.S. Department of Defense (headquartered at the Pentagon) has long dreamed of a robotic army. In early 2003, robots were sent to Iraq and Afghanistan to dig up roadside bombs, search caves, and guard weapons depots. Battle-ready robots were also sent to Iraq in 2005 to actually join the fighting.

These robots, known as SWORDS (Special Weapons Observation Reconnaissance Detection Systems) carry guns. They move along on wheels similar to those on a tank, rolling right over rocks and barbed wire.

The robots run on a special kind of battery and can operate for up to four hours at a time. From a remote location, human soldiers work the robots using control units with two joysticks, a few buttons, and a video screen. Developers say that controllers may eventually use virtual reality goggles instead of joysticks.

Pentagon officials point out that soldier robots don't care what the weather is like. They don't need food or clothes. They don't get bored or scared or lonely for their families. And although gunfire or bombs can damage the expensive units, they don't suffer pain or death. Research on robotic soldiers continues, in the hope that replacing human soldiers on the battlefield will save lives.

TIMELINE

A.D. 600 Callinicus invents "Greek fire."

850 Chinese chemists invent gunpowder.

1000 Chinese inventors design the first gun.

1200s Roger Bacon writes down the formula for gunpowder.

1300s The firelock is invented. Cannons and guns begin to show up on the European battlefield.

1427 Italians invent the first hand grenade.

1450 The matchlock is introduced.

1515 The wheel lock makes its appearance.

1610 Marin le Bourgeoys invents the flintlock.

1620 Leather guns are introduced, but they don't last long.

1775 David Bushnell tries to blow up a British warship with an underwater bomb.

1787 The Second Amendment to the U.S. Constitution guarantees citizens the right to keep and bear arms.

1794 The U.S. Congress establishes the Springfield (Massachusetts) Armory.

1835 Samuel Colt applies for a patent for his revolver.

1846 Ascanio Sobrero invents nitroglycerin.

1862 Richard Gatling invents the first machine gun.

1867 Alfred Nobel receives a patent for dynamite.

1883 Hiram Maxim invents the first automatic machine gun.

1904 TNT is used as an explosive for the first time.

1911 The Colt .38, the first American semiautomatic pistol, becomes the official U.S. military sidearm.

1915 Germans attack French troops with chlorine gas at Ypres, Belgium.

1917 Hugo Schmeisser designs the first submachine gun, the Bergmann Mashinen Pistole 18. German U-boats (submarines) sink 430 ships with torpedoes. The German army uses mustard gas on enemy troops.

1920 John Thompson invents his submachine gun (the tommy gun).

1925 The Geneva Protocol outlaws the use of chemical and biological weapons.

1936 Gerhard Schrader develops tabun.

1939 German scientists make the first batch of sarin gas.

1940 The German Luftwaffe bombs London and southern England, trying to destroy British factories and shipping operations.

1941 Nazis first use Zyklon-B to gas prisoners in the Gross-Rosen concentration camp in Poland.

1945 The U.S. military drops atomic bombs on the Japanese cities of Hiroshima and Nagasaki.

1962 Soviet and U.S. forces confront each other during the Cuban missile crisis, coming close to nuclear war.

1970 Treaty on the Non-Proliferation of Nuclear Weapons goes into effect.

1988 Saddam Hussein kills five thousand Kurds with mustard, cyanide, and nerve gases.

1991 Inspectors in Iraq uncover forty-six thousand chemical shells and warheads. Iraq admits to having a biological weapons lab.

2003 The U.S. military sends robotic equipment to Iraq and Afghanistan to assist troops.

2005 The U.S. military sends battle-ready robots to Iraq. A presidential commission reports that the United States is not prepared for a biological attack.

Glossary

atomic bomb: a powerful bomb fueled by splitting the nuclei of uranium or plutonium atoms

automatic weapon: a weapon that fires continuously as long as the trigger is held down

biological weapon: a weapon that releases deadly bacteria, viruses, or fungi

dynamite: an explosive made by mixing the chemical nitroglycerin with a stabilizing material such as wood pulp

gunpowder: an explosive made from saltpeter (potassium nitrate), sulfur, and carbon

missiles: in modern weaponry, self-propelled projectiles, such as guided or ballistic missiles, that carry explosives to a specific target

projectile: an object (such as a bullet) propelled forward by an outside force (such as the explosion of gunpowder)

rifle: a gun with spiral grooves cut into the inside of its barrel

semiautomatic weapon: a gun that automatically reloads itself but which must be fired by pulling the trigger each time

TNT: trinitrotoluene, a chemical compound that explodes when confined (as in mines or artillery shells)

warhead: the part of a missile that contains the explosive

World War I: from 1914 to 1918, a military conflict between the Allied powers (Great Britain, France, Russia, the United States, Japan, and others) and the Central powers (Germany, Austria-Hungary, and the Ottoman Empire)

World War II: from 1939 to 1945, a military conflict between the Allies (Great Britain, France, the USSR, the United States, and others) and the Axis powers (Germany, Italy, Japan, and others)

SELECTED BIBLIOGRAPHY

Campbell, Christy. *Weapons of War*. New York: Peter Bedrick Books, 1983.

Centers for Disease Control and Prevention. *Emergency Preparedness and Response*. April 2005. http://www.bt.cdc.gov/ (May 4, 2005).

Harris, Robert, and Jeremy Paxman. *A Higher Form of Killing*. New York: Hill and Wang, 1982.

Hogg, Ian. *The Weapons That Changed the World*. New York: Arbor House, 1986.

Mayor, Adrienne. *Greek Fire, Poison Arrows & Scorpion Bombs*. Woodstock, NY: Overlook Duckworth, 2003.

National Museum of the United States Air Force. March 2005. http://www.wpafb.af.mil/museum/index.htm (April 27, 2005).

O'Connell, Robert L. *Soul of the Sword*. New York: The Free Press, 2002.

Spiers, Edward M. *Chemical Warfare*. Chicago: University of Illinois Press, 1986.

Tunis, Edwin. *Weapons*. Cleveland: The World Publishing Company, 1954.

Volkman, Ernest. *Science Goes to War*. New York: John Wiley & Sons, 2002.

Weiner, Tim. "A New Model Army Soldier Rolls Closer to Battle." *The New York Times Online*. February 16, 2005. http://www.nytimes.com.

Young, Peter. *The Machinery of War*. New York: Crescent Books, 1983.

FURTHER READING AND WEBSITES

Allen, John. *High-Tech Weapons*. San Diego: Blackbirch Press, 2005.
Beginning with World War II, this book looks at the impacts technology
has on how wars are fought.

Dartford, Mark. *Bombers*. Minneapolis: Lerner Publications Company, 2003.
Dartford details modern and historic bomber planes, with black-and-white
and color photographs.

———. *Missiles and Rockets*. Minneapolis: Lerner Publications Company,
2003.
Using a variety of photographs, this book looks at modern and historic missiles and rockets and how those weapons are used in battle.

Feldman, Ruth Tenzer. *World War I*. Minneapolis: Lerner Publications
Company, 2004.
Feldman's coverage includes information on the weapons and gases used
during World War I.

FirstWorldWar.com
http://www.firstworldwar.com/index.htm
This site looks in detail at "the war to end all wars." Articles explain
weapons, battles, and trench warfare, with links to propaganda, primary
sources, vintage photographs, and other information.

Gay, Kathlyn. *Silent Death*. Brookfield, CT: Twenty-First Century Books, 2001.
Gay presents an explanation of the damage that results from biological and
chemical warfare and how modern world powers are working against the
development and use of these weapons.

Goldstein, Margaret J. *World War II: Europe*. Minneapolis: Lerner
Publications Company, 2004.
Goldstein's book covers weapons technology developed for European
ground, air, and sea battles.

HistoryforKids.org
http://www.historyforkids.org
The History for Kids website provides links to stories of ancient warfare, including the Persian Wars and the Punic Wars.

"Jump Back in Time." *The Library of Congress*
http://www.americaslibrary.gov/cgi-bin/page.cgi/jb
The Library of Congress's Jump Back in Time feature supplies historical background for America's conflicts, from the Revolution through World War II. Each topic's coverage includes links to detailed articles.

Long, Barbara. *Gun Control and the Right to Bear Arms*. Springfield, NJ: Enslow Publishers, 2002.
Long presents both sides of the hotly debated topic of government control of the ownership of guns.

Rivera, Sheila. *Weapons of Mass Destruction*. Minneapolis: Abdo & Daughters Publishing, 2003.
As part of the World in Conflict: The Middle East series, this book uses photographs, diagrams, and a timeline to detail the development and use of WMD in that region.

Sherman, Josepha. *The Cold War*. Minneapolis: Lerner Publications Company, 2004.
Sherman charts the development of nuclear weapons during the course of the Cold War.

Woods, Michael, and Mary B. Woods. *Ancient Warfare*. Minneapolis: Runestone Press, 2000.
Ancient Warfare looks at the development of weapons and strategies from the Stone Age through the Roman Empire.

Cover and Chapter Opener Photo Captions

Cover Top: A soldier stands next to a cannon on the deck of the gunboat *Hunchback*. Bottom: A Tomahawk cruise missile

pp. 4–5 This illustration depicts a Neanderthal holding a primitive weapon of stone and wood.

p. 6 This painting shows an ancient Greek city burning, perhaps set aflame with a firearm known as Greek fire.

p. 18 Dynamite sticks have many uses beyond warfare. They can be used to blast out mines, damsites, and building foundations.

p. 26 U.S. soldiers surround a Gatling gun in the Philippines in the late 1800s.

p. 33 A mushroom cloud appears after the testing of a thermonuclear bomb in the Marshall Islands in 1950.

pp. 46–47 A U.S. Navy robot carries an explosive-deterring device in its claws during a military exercise.

About the Author

Born in Baltimore, Maryland, Judith Herbst grew up in Queens, New York. Before becoming a full-time writer, she was an English teacher. Her first book for kids was *Sky Above and Words Beyond*. Her other books include the Unexplained series (*Aliens, Beyond the Grave, ESP, Hoaxes, Monsters*, and *UFOs*) and *The History of Transportation*.

Photo Acknowledgments

The images in this book are used with the permission of: Montgomery Ward & Co., p. 1 and borders throughout; © Bettmann/CORBIS, pp. 4–5, 15, 20; © Archivo Iconografico, S.A./CORBIS, p. 6; © Hulton Archive/Getty Images, p. 9; National Parks Service, p. 10; Library of Congress, p. 12 (LC-USZ62-8623); © Underwood & Underwood/CORBIS, p. 18; National Archives, War and Conflict Collection, pp. 23, 24, 28, 29, 40; © CORBIS, pp. 26, 33, 42; © John Springer Collection/CORBIS, p. 31; © Hulton-Deutsch Collection/CORBIS, p. 35; © Yomiuri Shibun/CORBIS SYGMA, p. 37; Navy News Service, pp. 46–47;

Front cover: National Archives, War and Conflict Collection (top); © Reuters/CORBIS (bottom). Back cover: Montgomery Ward & Co.